ISBN-13: 978-1500621469
ISBN-10: 1500621463
Academy for Adolescent Health, Inc.
410 N. Main Street
Washington, PA 15301
1 (888) 301 2311 - podmj@healthyteens.com

Nonnie

talks about Gender

An Interactive Coloring Book for Children and Adults

Written by Dr. Mary Jo Podgurski
Illustrations by Alice M. Burroughs

Dedication:

For Jai and her wonderful parents. You are my heart.

For all the amazing young people who teach me about gender,
gender identity, and personhood through their lives.
I am grateful for your wisdom and courage.

Thank you again, artist Alice Burroughs.
Your talent reaches everyone.

With special gratitude to my outstanding consultants:
My Family:
(Rich, Amy, Paul, Lisa, Evan, Nate and Erin)
Amanda Campbell

Dr. Betsy Crane

Joan Garrity

Dr. Eli R. Green

Maureen Kelly

Sam Killermann

Dr. James M. Longo

Anne E. Lynch

Luca Maurer

Emmett A. Patterson
Dr. Elizabeth Schroeder

Danny Shaffer

Al Vernacchio

C.S. Vincent

Jean Workman

Thank you to Robbi Linton for coloring the cover picture.
Special thanks for the Pro Athlete photo on page 26 to
Lindsey Cain, MEd. Pittsburgh Passion Offensive Tackle
Photos purchased from Dreamstime.com

*Sometimes the questions are complicated
and the answers are simple.*

Dr. Seuss

*Unless someone like you cares a whole awful lot,
nothing is going to get better. It's not.*

Dr. Seuss

*Today you are you, that is truer than true.
There is no one alive that is youer than you.*

Dr. Seuss

Think and wonder. Wonder and think.

Dr. Seuss

Words from Colleagues about
Nonnie Talks about Gender
(please see the back cover for more)

With specialized expertise, along with heaping portions of patience and kindness, Nonnie Talks About Gender explains important concepts, while underlining the most important of all - that all people should be treated with dignity and respect. I wish my Nonnie had had this book when I was growing up - thanks to Dr. Podgurski, now every child's nonna (and their parents, caregivers, teachers, and friends) can have it!

Luca Maurer, Ithaca College LGBT Education
Outreach & Services Program Director, Counseling and Wellness

Dr. Podgurski – AKA "Nonnie" – has written a simple book about an extremely complex subject, gender. In light of much recent attention in the media to the confusing and sometimes scary subject of gender diversity and variation, adults who wisely choose to not ignore or minimize children's inquiries, are often at a loss as to how to begin. This book is a gift to parents and educators wanting some help in answering such questions; questions about what they may be hearing, or seeing, or experiencing for themselves. The pre-adolescent's evolving sense of personal identity and fairly concrete thinking does indeed make for a tough time figuring all this out! (Not to mention the tough time had by many, many adults...)

Dr. P is known in the field of sexuality education for her endless innovation in teaching sexuality education to children, adolescents and to adults. With sweet black and white drawings illustrating the journey of learning of the two main characters, Tamika and Alex, and bright graphics that encourage creative interaction with these new and difficult concepts, Nonnie Talks About Gender is a charming, respectful, honest and accessible introduction to a truly challenging topic.

Joan Garrity, *Principal Garrity Health Consulting & Training*

Gender is a tough subject for adults to discuss between them. It's even harder to try to explain gender to kids. Dr. Podgurski's book does the work for you by taking a very complicated topic and making it understandable for younger children.

Elizabeth Schroeder, EdD, MSW
Sexuality Education Expert

This book is written in a friendly, but incisive way that engages you in an internal dialogue about your own identity, while seeing one way that the conversation might play out. It has much to offer both children and adults. There is no one way to teach gender, but you can't go wrong with Mary Jo's approach rooted in respect and empathy. So much of the confusion I experienced in my adolescent years would have been put to ease in an afternoon at Nonnie's house.

Sam Killermann, Author of
The Social Justice Advocate's Handbook: A Guide to Gender

Children are full of questions as a general rule, and seem to be even more so if presented with information which goes beyond their normal sphere. Dr. Podgurski has taken on the challenging task of discussing gender and, even more courageously, gender non-conformity, and transformed it into an accessible, honest, and fun read. This should be on every modern parent's or guardian's bookshelf.

Anne E. Lynch, Manager of Operations,
Three Rivers Community Foundation

In "Nonnie Talks About Gender," Mary Jo Podgurski has created an engaging book for children and an empowering guide for parents on an important, and complex topic. A strength of the book is the way parents are encouraged to modify their reading of the book to suit their child. There is much for children to like - the coloring pages, the questions, and the colorful graphics. Background information for parents will help them guide their children's understanding.

Betsy Crane, Ph.D., Professor,
Center for Human Sexuality Studies, Widener University

The creative interaction of the book encourages a respectful dialogue that sets the stage for the early and often conversations parents and trusted adults should have about difficult topics.

Jean Workman, MA, Family Life and Sexuality Education Specialist
Children's Aid Society-Carrera Adolescent Pregnanc Prevention Program

Gender identity is fallaciously simplified to the point of offense, and worse, for those who aren't cisgender. This book facilitates a respectful and inclusive conversation on gender, to clarify its truly expansive spectrum for parents and children alike.

Amanda Campbell, *Alumni, Peer Educator*

HOW TO USE THIS BOOK:

For Children (page 1):

Nonnie Talks about Gender was created to be used by children and adults together. Please read this book with someone who matters to you.

1. This book is very special. You are in charge of how much you read and whether or not you play the learning games. It's up to you!

2. A What do YOU think? page is a great page to help people talk with each other. Please talk with a trusted adult. Please listen!

3. The book is divided into chapters. You decide how quickly you want to read the chapters. If you feel that too many words are going into your head or you have too many questions...

You could take a break, stop a while, and read the rest of the book later.

 If you take a break you could stand up and stretch..

 Or have a snack...

Lungs
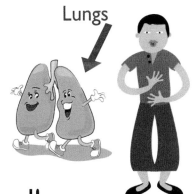

Or take some deep breaths...

 Or even run around!

4. This picture means you may color the page if you wish.

5. *This symbol means a word may be new. The Glossary on pages 54 and 55 will help with new words.

Most important:
Every person is different. Each child who picks up this book is different. Each adult who reads this book with a child is different. Some ideas may be easy to understand. That's OK. Some ideas may be hard to understand. That's OK, too.

HOW TO USE THIS BOOK:

For Parents, Teachers and Trusted Adults:

I don't consider myself an expert on gender; so much about gender is individual. People are dynamic. We're each unique. I did my best to make a vibrant, alive, concept as concrete as possible for children. I do think I am a pretty good nonnie, though. I consider teaching my vocation, not my job. I am deeply grateful for my wonderful consultants who freely shared their wisdom. I send you joy!

1. The book is divided into nine chapters. The chapters are only suggestions— they divide the content to allow for pleasant learning. The book should be read at your own pace—it's up to you. You know your children best. Please monitor their attention, their interest, and their awareness/understanding of the concepts.

2. Please check in with your children to ascertain their readiness to move forward after each chapter.

3. Nonnie Talks about Gender addresses complicated concepts. The ideas of empathy, society, and respect are introduced to help children deal with difference. More information for parents/teachers/trusted adults is on pages 56 and 57.

4. The What do YOU think? pages should be completed at a child's pace, but are important. Learning takes place when we process information.

Most important:

Please be aware of the "music" behind your words (thanks to Pam Wilson who first taught me that concept). Adult modeling and acceptance of issues like respect are vital. Emerson said: "What you do speaks so loudly I cannot hear what you say." Children watch adults. Adults matter to children. Please honor diversity and teach respect. Thank you.

Nelson Mandela said: "No one is born hating another person because of the color of his skin, or his background, or his religion. People must learn to hate, and if they can learn to hate, they can be taught to love, for love comes more naturally to the human heart than its opposite."

Did you ever have a
huge question?

Most children are curious about a lot of different things.

Would you like to read a story
about two children with lots of
questions? The story may answer some
of your questions.

If you still have questions when the story is finished,
please ask your parents or a
trusted adult.

A boy named Alex and a girl named Tamika were best friends.

They couldn't remember a time when they weren't friends.

Their parents said they were even in the same play group when they were only two years old!

Tamika is an only child but Alex has a baby sister named Alisha. He loves his sister.

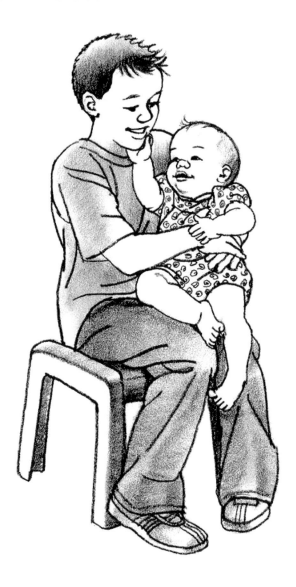

Tamika loves Alisha too and is a big part of her life.

Both Alex and Tamika are excited.

Soon Alisha will be a year old!
Alex and Tamika have planned a birthday party.

Alisha was happy when Tamika gave
her a birthday present!

When she opened it Alex was confused.

The present was a baby doll.

Alex said, "Thanks for the present, Mika, but Alisha likes to play ball with me."

"She likes to play with blocks."

"She likes to pound things."

"She loves trains."

"Alisha likes to pull things, too."

"She doesn't like to play with baby dolls."

Tamika was a little bit angry and a lot confused.
"She can still do stuff with you," she said, "but Alisha is a girl."

"So…" said Alex.
"So girls play with baby dolls," Tamika said.
Alex frowned. "Yeah, but girls can play with toys for boys and boys can play with toys for girls, right?"

"I don't know. Why are there toys just for boys or just for girls? When I went shopping the toy store was divided into a boy area and a girl area. Why is that?"

Alex could see Tamika was getting more confused.
"What if a girl doesn't want to play with toys for girls, like Alisha?" Alex asked. "I'm a boy and I never wanted to play with baby dolls."

"Huh?"

Now they were
both confused.

"I know," Tamika said, "let's ask my mom." Tamika's mom is a nurse and they often ask her questions. They spend lots of time learning with her.

Then Tamika remembered. Her mom was at work.

Alex said: "Let's ask my dad."

Alex's dad smiled. "I think you should ask your Nonnie," he said. She can answer questions about gender."

What questions do you think Alex would want to ask his dad?

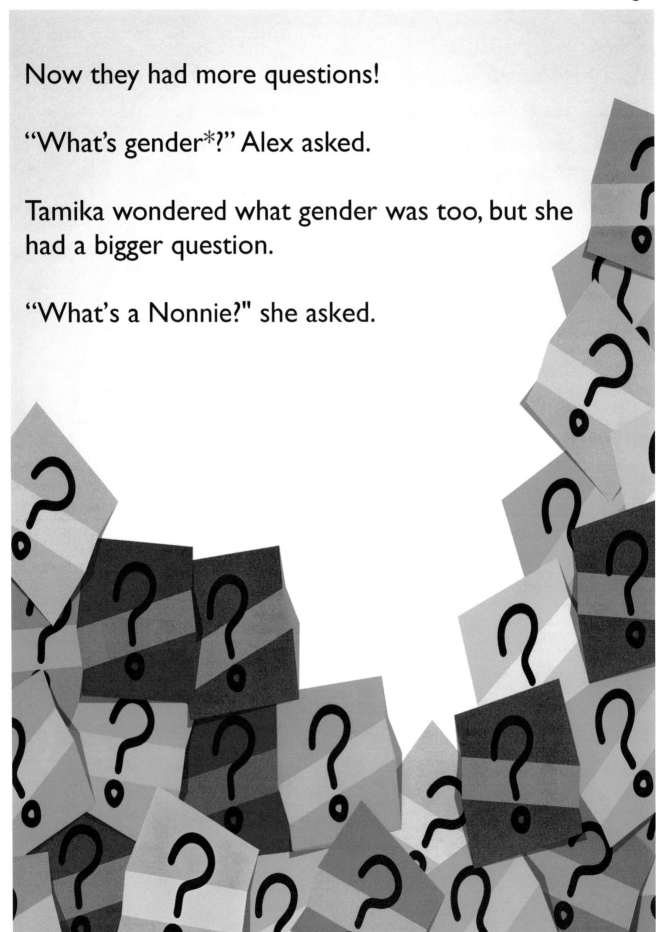

Now they had more questions!

"What's gender*?" Alex asked.

Tamika wondered what gender was too, but she had a bigger question.

"What's a Nonnie?" she asked.

"That's an easy question, Mika." Alex looked pleased.
He knew an answer!
"A nonnie is a grandmother."

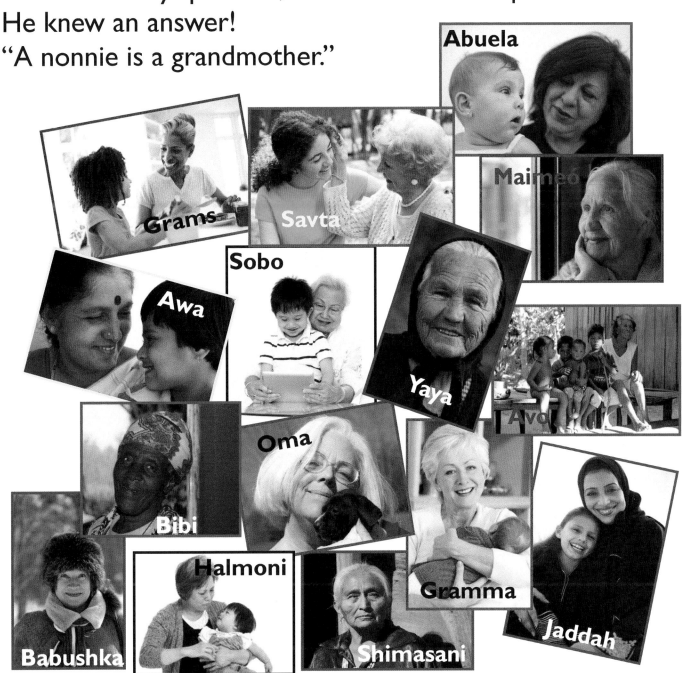

Alex's dad agreed. "Our family calls Alex and Alisha's
grandma Nonnie. Many people in many societies* have
different names for grandmother.
What do you call your grandma, Tamika?"

Tamika laughed. "Meme."

"Our Nonnie was supposed to be called 'nonna' but I made the word into 'nonnie' when I was a baby," Alex explained.

"Nonnie is a teacher. Great idea, Dad! She can answer our questions."

First Alex's dad called Tamika's mom to ask if the children could ask Nonnie questions. The answer was 'yes'.

Then they drove to Nonnie's house. After she fed them sandwiches and cookies and fruit (Nonnie always feeds people), the children sat at the table.

They were quiet for a while, then Tamika started to fidget, and finally Alex said, "Nonnie, we're a little bit nervous. We have some questions but we don't know how to ask."

Nonnie smiled. "I have a book," she said, "and crayons and paper. Let's talk."

"Before I answer your questions," Nonnie said, "I'd like to make you some promises. I think you won't feel as nervous after I do. Is that OK?"

The children said "yes" together and then grinned when they said it at the same time.

Nonnie said, "I promise to answer all your questions honestly. I will tell you the truth."

"I promise to respect you and respect everything you say. No question you ask me will make me lose respect for you."

"I promise to really listen to you."

"I promise to stop and take a break any time you want."

Nonnie asked. "Can you think of any other promises you'd like me to make to you?" The children said, "No."

Tamika and Alex liked Nonnie's promises.

Do you like these promises? Why or why not?

Alex looked at Tamika and Tamika looked at Alex. Then the children took big breaths and a bunch of questions tumbled out of both of their mouths!

"Does Alisha need to play with baby dolls?"

"Is it ok if she plays with the toys boys like?"

"Why are there toys just for boys and toys just for girls—like in a kids' meal?"

"What happens if

a boy likes girl toys? Is that OK? Or if a girl likes boy toys?"

"Clothes are different for boys and girls too, but the rules about clothes seem different if you're a boy or a girl. Girls can wear clothes a boy might wear but a boy can't wear a dress, right? Why?

And the biggest question of all:

"What is gender?"

Nonnie said. "I will answer all your great questions.

I want you to promise me something.
I want you to promise that you will think.
I want you to use your brains like computers and think when we talk about something new."

"I also want you to use your heart when you're thinking. We will talk about gender and you will learn new words. Talking about gender may also make you feel things."

The children promised.

Then Alex asked, "Why would we feel things?"

Nonnie smiled. "Good thinking, Alex. We may feel things because gender is very personal. Respecting a person's gender is important but it might be confusing." Alex frowned. "Respect?" he asked.

Nonnie said: "Let's create a What do you think page."

15

Nonnie asked, "What do you think the word 'respect' means? She asked the children to draw a picture or write their thoughts on a piece of paper.

The children thought and thought, then they created a What do you think page.

What do you think the word 'respect' means?

Please draw or write your thoughts

©2014 ~ All rights reserved

Tamika said: "Respect is when you like people just the way they are."

Alex shook his head. "I don't think you need to like people to respect them. I think respect is how you treat someone."

"Yes," Tamika agreed. "But isn't respect also how you feel about someone?"

Nonnie was pleased. "Exactly right.
Respect is about feelings and about actions.
When you respect people you think positive things about them.
You act in a way that shows you care about their feelings.
You care whether or not they're OK.

We are respectful when we treat others as if they are people of worth*."

Do you agree?
Why or why not?

You can respect yourself.
Respecting yourself is really important.

YOU ARE IMPORTANT!

Alex frowned. "If that's respect then Mrs. Tate at school isn't respectful of some kids. She makes fun of them."

Nonnie looked sad, but then smiled. "People of all ages can be disrespectful," she said. "People of all ages can be taught respect. Let's play a learning game. Read each story below and decide if the people are respectful or not respectful."

What do YOU think?

1. A boy is at the movies and sees a friend enter the theatre. He texts the friend on his cell phone. The phone lights up and bothers the people seated around him.

_____ Respectful
_____ Not Respectful

2. A new boy comes to school. You don't like the way he is always studying. You keep your thoughts to yourself and don't make fun of him.

_____ Respectful
_____ Not Respectful

3. A boy in your grade is having a birthday party. He asks you to buy him a doll. You don't understand but you tell your parents to buy one anyway.

_____ Respectful
_____ Not Respectful

4. Someone on your sports team misses a really big play. You stomp off the field and call the person a bad name.

_____ Respectful
_____ Not Respectful

Tamika asked "I get that respect is important, but I still want to know...what exactly is gender? And is respect connected to gender?"

Nonnie looked happy! "Tamika, I love the way your brain is working!" she said. "Yes, respect is connected to gender. Gender is a little complicated*."

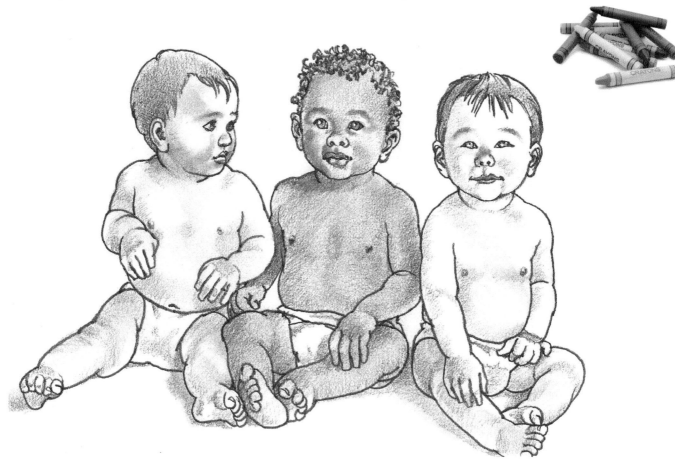

"When a baby is born someone shouts:

"It's a boy!" or "It's a girl!"

Hospitals often give new baby girls pink hats and new baby boys are often given blue hats."

"I get it!" Alex was excited. "Gender is whether a person is a girl or a boy."

"Like us!" Tamika said. "I'm a girl and you're a boy."

"Gender is different than that," Nonnie said.

"We sometimes think that whether a person is a girl or a boy is about biology*.

Boys and girls are born with different body parts. Gender is how people are taught they're supposed to act because of those body parts."

Alex was quiet while he thought about Nonnie's words. "Who tells kids how they're supposed to act?" he asked.

"Does it start with baby boys wearing blue and baby girls wearing pink?" Tamika asked. "Last summer we went to see my dad's family in Canada. Is gender the same everywhere?"

"A person's society* can tell kids how their gender is supposed to act, Alex. Each society is different, Tamika. I think it's time we create a What do you think page."

Nonnie asked, "What do you think the word 'society' means?"

The children thought and thought, then they created a new page.

What do YOU think the word 'society' means?

Please draw
or write your
thoughts

Tamika said, "Maybe a society is a bunch of people who live together."

Alex added, "People who have the same laws?"

Tamika agreed. "What about people who believe in the same things.
My meme talks about our church society."

Alex nodded. "Maybe people from the same country, who speak the same language."

"You're both correct." Nonnie smiled. "Societies can affect the way we act."

"Societies can be big or small. Societies can affect gender, especially gender roles*. Your questions about toys and kids' meals and clothes are all about gender roles."

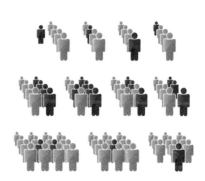

When the children were quiet, Nonnie asked, "How does talking about society make you curious?"

"We can live in more than one society at a time, can't we?" Tamika grinned and Alex added, "Like our family and our country. And our school." Nonnie agreed.

Before Nonnie could say What do you think? Tamika said, "We need to think about what the words 'gender roles' mean, right?"

The children thought and thought. They were getting good at creating What do you think pages!

What do YOU think the words 'gender roles' mean?

Please draw or write your thoughts

Alex almost jumped up and down with excitement. "Gender roles are why Tamika bought a baby doll for my sister. Alisha's a girl so people in our society say her gender role means she plays with a doll."

Nonnie smiled. "Yes, Alex. Gender roles can mean a boy or man should do certain things and a girl or woman should do certain things."

Tamika said, "It seemed like a doll was the right present." "It wasn't wrong, Tamika," Nonnie pointed to pictures in the book. "These children are playing with their toys based on traditional* gender roles."

"These children are playing with their toys based on non-traditional* gender roles."

"Like Alisha playing ball," said Tamika. Then she frowned. "I play soccer. So does Alex. Is soccer for boys or girls?"

"Both!" Alex couldn't imagine playing soccer without Tamika.

"Soccer is for both of you in today's world." Nonnie thought a minute. "American society has changed since I was your age," she said. "When I was a girl my friends and I jumped rope. There were no organized* sports for girls. Societies can change."

Nonnie showed the children a picture in the book. "Do you think it's OK for a boy to paint?" she asked.

Both children agreed - it was OK for anyone to paint.

"This picture shows a girl playing ball. How do you feel about girls playing sports?" Nonnie asked.

Nonnie was not surprised when both children thought girls playing sports was fine.

"It's cool," Tamika said. "I like sports. I'm glad society changed."

"Are gender roles changing for grown ups, too?"
Alex wondered.

What do YOU think?

Homemaker

Lawyer

Cook

Engineer

Child Care

Nonnie said, "I'm glad you asked. Let's play another learning game. Look at each picture. Do these jobs show traditional gender roles? Why or why not?"

Florist

Pilot

Pro Athlete

Nurse   Soldier

Both children looked closely at the pictures."Do you think people should pick jobs they like?" Nonnie asked.

"I think so. I've seen men cook before," Alex said, "although mostly my dad and grandpa. Grandpa makes great spaghetti, right Nonnie?"

Nonnie agreed, then Tamika laughed. "My mom says grilling outside doesn't count as cooking. Mom says cooking means making breakfast and sometimes fixing dinner at the end of the day too!"

Nonnie said, "When your dad and aunts were growing up, Alex, we all had fun cooking!"

"I've seen women play basketball but I've never seen a pro football player who was a woman." Alex smiled at Tamika. "Maybe you'll be a pro quarterback someday, Mika."

"I won't have time for that, Alex," Tamika's grin was huge. "I'll be too busy being president."

Alex shook his head. "Nonnie," he said. "You said gender was a little complicated. It seems pretty simple to me."

"It can be simple, Alex. Let's talk about people. People are all different, right? People are different not only in the way they look but also in the way they act."

Both children agreed. Alex said, "Like teachers. I know. Mrs. Tate is different from Mr. Bennet. He's the other third grade teacher. He never makes fun of kids. I hope I get in Mr. Bennet's room next school year."

Nonnie hugged Alex and whispered, "Me too." Then she asked Tamika, "Did your present come in a box, Mika?"

Tamika was proud. "It did. I wrapped it myself."

Nonnie asked to see the box, and Tamika looked around. "It was like that box," Tamika said, pointing to a box holding books. It was a pretty traditional box. It looked like many other boxes.

"Interesting," said Nonnie. "Do you think all boxes are the same?"

What do YOU think?

"Is it OK if boxes are all different?" Nonnie asked.

The children thought it was OK.

"What if people are a little like boxes," Nonnie said, "each one is different. Each one is OK. What's important is what's inside the box."

"Gender can be very different for each person. Not everyone's gender fits into two boxes! Sometimes people put 'boy' or 'girl' labels* on boxes and think everyone will fit into them."

Nonnie smiled at Tamika and Alex.

"May I ask you a personal question? It's OK if you decide not to answer it."
The children said a question was OK.

You may draw yourself in the mirror if you wish.

Nonnie asked the children what they see when they look in a mirror.

What do you see when you look in a mirror?

"What do you see?" Nonnie asked.

"I see me," Alex said.

"Me too," said Tamika.

Nonnie nodded and asked, "Would you change anything about the person you see in the mirror?"

Alex thought a minute. "I'd like to be taller."

Tamika laughed, "Me too," she said. "We'd better practice shooting hoops, Alex. A lot of kids are taller than us."

Alex agreed, then added, "I wish I had fewer freckles."

When Tamika said, "I think your freckles are OK." Alex felt happy.

Tamika paused. "I'd like my hair to be less curly."

When Alex said, "I like your hair just the way it is," Tamika felt happy.

Nonnie told both children they were amazing just the way they were.

Nonnie listened carefully as the children talked about the way they saw themselves in the mirror. Then she asked very gently, "What if you saw yourself as a different gender."

"Is that possible?" Alex asked, but Tamika was quiet. She waited to hear what Nonnie would say.

"Yes, it is possible," Nonnie pointed to two words in her book.

Gender Identity

The book read:

Gender identity refers to the way people see themselves and the gender with which people identify*.

"Gender identity can be different for each person," Nonnie said. "It's about what a person feels on the inside. Sometimes gender identity will match what a person sees in the mirror and sometimes it will not."

"What if a person looks in the mirror and sees a different gender?" Nonnie asked. "Or a person may feel like a boy sometimes and a girl sometimes. Look at this picture," Nonnie pointed to a picture in her book. "One name for someone's gender identity when a person feels like a mix of boy and girl is gender fluid*."

Alex looked the way he did when Mrs. Tate asked him to do his times tables….like he was thinking very hard. He wasn't thinking about the new words gender fluid. He was imagining the way the boy might feel when he looked in the mirror. Then he sighed. "Wow! I really would like to lose the freckles but I never felt I was a girl. What if people don't understand how the boy feels? What if people aren't nice?"

 Nonnie was so proud of Alex she gave him a huge hug. "Excellent, Alex. You don't really understand all of this, and that's OK. You respect each person. You're developing empathy*."

"And empathy is?" Tamika asked, and then laughed. "It's weird, Nonnie. Learning with you is like playing dominos. One thing leads to another."

 Now Nonnie gave Tamika a huge hug! Then she said, "When people don't understand how others are different, they may feel afraid. When people are afraid they may not be nice. Learning about respect and empathy is important when we talk about gender."

"Tell us about empathy," Tamika said.

"Empathy is tough to explain but I believe you are old enough to understand. Alex, do you remember when you were losing your two front teeth and one wouldn't come out no matter how you wiggled it?"

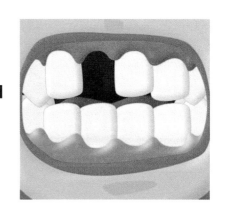

Both children remembered. "It hurt. I couldn't eat apples." Alex made a sad face, and Tamika nodded. "You were pretty cranky until they came out," she said.

"Tamika, did you understand how it felt to have two loose front teeth?" Nonnie asked, and Tamika shook her head. "Not until I lost my own two front teeth," she said.

"Then you understood?"

Tamika nodded.

Alex looked at Tamika and Tamika looked at Alex. Finally, Alex said, "So….empathy is about teeth. And maybe apples."

"Not exactly," Nonnie continued. "Alex, I remember how you felt when Alisha was going to be born. Is it OK to talk about that feeling?"

Since Tamika had been a big part of Alex's life then, he agreed. "I was scared."

"You felt angry, too." Tamika added.

"My mom said it was OK to feel angry and scared. She told me feelings were OK. She helped me talk about them." He thought about his sister and shrugged. "I love Alisha now."

"You're right, Alex. Feelings are OK." Nonnie looked at Tamika. "You helped Alex, didn't you, Mika?"

Tamika remembered. "You thought the new baby would mess up your life, Alex. I could imagine feeling like that if my mom and dad brought home a new baby."

"You imagined what Alex was feeling, Tamika. You had empathy for his feelings."

"Why is empathy important when we talk about gender?" Alex asked.

"Do you remember when we talked about boxes?" Nonnie asked.

"I said not everyone's gender fits into two boxes - one for boys and one for girls."

The children remembered. "The boy looking in the mirror doesn't fit into a 'boy' box, right?" Tamika asked.

"The boy would be different," Alex said. Tamika could tell Alex was thinking because he was quieter than normal.

"Remember we said that when people don't understand or are afraid of difference they may not be respectful. They may not treat others nicely. It's good if people have empathy and respect others. Empathy helps people think with their hearts."

Nonnie added, "You're both really listening. Do you want to take a break?" Both children said they were OK.

Both children looked at Nonnie, then Tamika said, "I still don't get it. Tell me again, what's empathy?"

Nonnie asked, "Have either of you ever felt like someone was mean to you?"

Alex answered quickly, "That big guy on the bus."

"He's a bully, Alex," Tamika reminded her friend. "He stopped bothering you last year."

"How did you feel when you knew Alex was not respected by someone, Tamika?"

"Mad for sure. Scared too," Tamika hugged Alex. "I was proud of Alex when he told Mr. Bennet."

"You understood how Alex felt, Tamika, even when no one was being mean to you." Nonnie waited while the children talked quietly to each other.

Suddenly Alex got it. "Is empathy understanding what someone else feels?"

"Trying to understand," Nonnie said. "And caring about how someone else is feeling."

"When I starting thinking what it might feel like if someone wasn't nice to another person because of gender...." Alex stopped, still thinking.

"You said Alex was developing empathy, Nonnie," Tamika finished. "I get it now. I do."

Both children were silent, then Nonnie asked, "Any other questions?"

Tamika was curious. "Does everyone have a gender identity?"

"Yes, Tamika." Nonnie thought about the best way to explain something as important as gender identity. "What if each person was different, just like each box we looked at was different?"

Tamika grinned. "I remember the picture of the cute dog, Nonnie." Tamika already had three dogs but she wanted more.

"We wouldn't know what was inside a box until we opened it, right?" Nonnie asked. "What if each person's gender identity is inside of them? We can't tell a person's gender identity from looking at the outside of the person, just like we wouldn't know these pets were inside the boxes until we looked inside." She pointed at the pictures and both children grinned.

Nonnie continued: "A person's gender identity is special to that person. It's personal. It may not match the outside of the person. We all need to develop empathy for gender identity."

Nonnie said, "Let's stop and think.

Is there anything about developing empathy for gender identity you're having trouble understanding? Let's create a What do you think page!"

What do YOU think about gender identity? Is it important to develop empathy for others?
Why or why not?

Please draw or write your thoughts

Nonnie looked carefully at both children. "Are you ready for more new words?" The children were ready.

Nonnie said, "I'm proud of you. Even some adults don't understand these words. Most people identify as cisgender*. When people identify as cisgender, their gender identity (the way people feel on the inside) is the same as their biology (body parts), and what they see when they look in a mirror."

Both children repeated the new word: "Cisgender."

 "What if the way people feel on the inside doesn't match what they see in the mirror?" Tamika asked. "Like the boy looking in the mirror in your book, Nonnie."

Nonnie answered, "The word used for a person's gender identity when it does not match biology (or what a person sees in the mirror) is transgender*." Tamika whispered, "transgender" so she would remember.

"If the boy in the picture saw himself as a girl when he looked in the mirror, would he identify as transgender?" Alex asked.

Before Nonnie could answer, Tamika said, "or he could identify as that other gender word."

For a moment Nonnie was confused, then she understood. "Gender fluid, Tamika," she said. "You're correct. The boy in the picture might identify as gender fluid - moving from one gender to another - or he might identify as transgender."

 Nonnie sighed. These ideas were new. She looked at Alex and Tamika very carefully. "Would you like to take a break?"

The children said they were OK. "We still have questions," Alex said.

Nonnie was pleased. "Listen carefully, then. Even names like gender fluid or cisgender can be placed on boxes. People may change. They may identify themselves differently as they change. I don't really like labels when they're used for people." She pulled a pack of gum from her purse.

 "I think labels are for things like gum, not people. Things cannot decide 'who' they are, but people can."

Alex thought a minute, then he said, "I don't think we need a label for someone as long as we respect the person. Right?"

Tamika agreed. "If people are happy with who they are, why do we need to give labels to them?"

HAPPY

Nonnie said, "You're both very right. We don't need to label people. If we're respectful of each person we can listen and learn from them."

 Suddenly Tamika grinned. "I like being a girl but I don't think I will follow all the rules for a girl's gender."

Alex laughed. "Mika, you never follow any kind of rules unless you have to."

 "I know. I've seen the size of the high heels some women wear. Ouch! I'm never wearing shoes like that."

Alex thought Tamika was funny. Nonnie nodded. "You're talking about gender expression*, Tamika - the way we show our gender identity by our clothes and the way we act. Imagine people showing their gender expression in different ways." For some reason the more the children thought the more they laughed about the high heels!

When they stopped giggling, Nonnie asked, "What do you want to learn next? " The children decided they needed to create a What do you think? page. They have a lot of thinking ahead!

What do YOU think about new words like cisgender, gender fluid and transgender?

Please draw or write your thoughts

The children talked about their what do you think page. Then Nonnie decided they looked a little tired. They'd learned a lot of new things! She suggested two ideas: playing a learning game and ice cream. Both were hits!

The learning game is about pronouns*. Nonnie explained: "A pronoun takes the place of a noun so a person doesn't need to repeat a name over and over.

Tamika, if you wanted to tell your mom about some fun things you did with Alex, you might say: *Alex and I had so much fun playing with his little sister. He loves to play blocks with Alisha, so we all played with blocks together.* The words 'he' and 'his' are pronouns. They take the place of saying the name Alex."

The children nodded.
They learned about pronouns in school.

"Most Americans use two types of gender pronouns:

he, him or **his** for boys/men and
she, her or **hers** for girls/women."

Here is the learning game if you want to play:

Draw a line to match a pronoun to each person.*

1. Sally identifies as a cisgender girl.

2. Sam identifies as a transgender boy.

3. Sandy identifies as a transgender girl.

4. Sean identifies as a cisgender boy.

5. Sardi identifies as agender.

He

She

Ze

They/Them

"Wait a minute," Tamika gave Nonnie the same look she had when she ate sour candy. "That's not fair. You never explained ze*. Or agender*."

Nonnie agreed. "You're right. Some people don't identify as a boy or as a girl. Those people may use the word agender to describe themselves. They may also use other words. Some people who identify as agender like to use the pronoun 'ze' or other pronouns like 'they' or 'them'."

Alex's face was more scrunched up than Tamika's. "I don't understand. I need to work on my empathy," he said.

Answers on page 57

"It's OK to not understand at first, as long as each person is treated with respect—as a person of worth.

The best way to understand others is by listening to them and learning about them."

Each person is a person of worth

"Now let's eat our ice cream!"

"One more thing, Nonnie," Alex said while eating his ice cream, "You said most people use two kinds of pronouns in American society. Are some societies different?"

"Yes," she answered.

"For example, some Native Americans, also called First Nation people, believe some people have Two Spirits*."

"Two Spirited people are considered very special in their society.

They show characteristics* that are masculine* (like the male gender) and feminine* (like the female gender)."

Alex asked, "Which pronoun would I use when speaking with a Two Spirited person?"

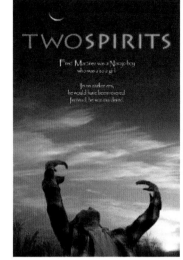

http://twospirits.org/

Nonnie smiled. "I think the best way to handle a situation where you don't know which pronoun to use is to simply ask the person respectfully."

Do you agree?
How can we respect each person?

Do you have any questions?

Ask your parent or a trusted adult.

The phone rang. It was Tamika's mom, calling to say she would pick the children up. They heard her say, "I'm guessing they won't need dinner, right Nonnie?"

Everyone seemed to know how Nonnie's house works.

Nonnie thought the children were amazing!
Alex and Tamika were happy they learned
so many new things. Are you?

What do YOU think about the new things you learned in this book?

Please write or draw three new things you learned.

Thank you for thinking!

Thank you for using your heart to think!

Please draw or write your thoughts

Agender: People who do not place a name to their gender. *My friend Sam doesn't feel like a boy or a girl. Ze identifies agender. (pg 49)*

Biology: The study of living things, including our bodies and how they work. *A person's biology includes height and the color of a person's eyes. (pg 18, 44)*

Characteristics: Something about a person that identifies that person. *My grandmother's kindness is one of her best characteristics. (pg 51)*

Cisgender: *Sounds like "Siss-gender"* A gender identity where self-identity is the same as body parts. *Most people identify as cisgender. (pg 44)*

Complicated: Not simple. *Alex thinks math is complicated. (pg 18, 30)*

Empathy: Understanding and sharing the feelings of another. *Shane found empathy for her niece's illness when she babysat her and the little girl didn't want to play. (pg 36—41)*

Feminine: Having qualities of or looking like a woman. *Laci loved to dress in feminine looking clothes with lots of ruffles. (pg 51)*

Gender: Roles, behavior and activities a society makes OK for men and women. *Gender can be different in the U.S. than in other countries. (pg 7 on)*

Gender Expression: Refers to the way people show their masculinity or femininity. It may include many things, like the way people dress, style their hair, or behaviors like speech. *Conor's gender expression includes enjoying nail polish and getting manicures. (pg 46)*

Gender Fluid: A gender identity that does not identify with either gender, but is more like a dynamic mix of boy and girl. May also be referred to as gender variant. *Terry loves to dress like a princess and also feels like a boy. Terry identifies as gender fluid. (pg 35)*

Gender Identity: Refers to the way people see themselves and the gender with which people identify. *Danny is happier now that his family is accepting of his gender identity of male. (pg 34)*

Labels: Something attached to a product to define it or give information about it. *Sam's dad read the label on the hot dogs before he bought them.* A person may be given a label connected to gender, like cisgender or transgender. *(pg 31)*

Identify: When you decide who you are. *Sasha identifies as a girl (pg 34)*

Masculine: Having qualities of or looking like a man. *Logan was surprised his little brother wasn't more masculine. (pg 51)*

Non-traditional: Not usually done—not a tradition. *A traditional wedding dress in China is red and in the U.S. a wedding dress is usually white. (pg 24)*

Organized: (In sports) teams established with rules, uniforms, and games, often in schools. *Sign ups for soccer were a great success and proved how well organized sports worked in their school. (pg 24)*

Pronouns: A word used in place of a noun. *Sally is glad she likes art. (pg 48)*

Societies: Groups of people with shared laws, traditions, and values. The word culture may be used in place of the word society. *Taylor lives in an American society. (pg 19)*

Traditional: Usually or often done; something historically common. *Grandma loves traditional meals like the one she serves on Thanksgiving. (pg 23)*

Transgender: A gender identity where a person's self-identity doesn't match body parts. *Some transgender children know they identify with a different gender when they are very young. (pg 44)*

Two Spirits: Words used to describe mixed gender people in Native traditions. *After watching the movie about Two Spirit people, Serena felt she understood the idea. (pg 50)*

Worth: Deserving effort, attention and respect. *Each person is worth our time and attention. (pg 16, 50)*

Ze: Along with other words like 'they', may be used as a pronoun for people who identify as agender. *Amanda would like us to use ze as a pronoun. (pg 49)*

Parent Information on Gender Identity

As parents we are also teachers. Knowledge is important to growth. Only parents can provide their family's values along with information.

Why teach about gender? We live in a changing world. Your child may have questions about gender as a result of changes in gender roles. Your child may encounter a classmate who is gender fluid—whose dress or behavior challenges traditional gender roles and gender expression. Your child may be gender fluid and need your support. Your other children may have questions about a sibling whose gender expression is unique.

I wrote *Nonnie Talks about Gender* to encourage adult/child communication on a potentially controversial issue. Each child is unique developmentally as well. Some of the concepts in the book may be too abstract for some children. Read the book with your child in sections if necessary. When responding to children's questions, please remember:

- Less is more. There's no need to explain adult concerns or issues. If told "Paul was not happy as a boy and is happy as a girl and would like to be called Paula" many children will simply accept that information.

- Not all girls like to play with "girl toys" and not all boys like to play with "boy toys". Children are very unique. Not all children fit into two boxes labeled "boy" or "girl".

- Gender identity refers to the way people see themselves and the gender with which people identify

- Some people confuse gender identity with sexual orientation. They are not the same. Sexual orientation is about attraction, gender identity is about identity.

- When a person's gender identity (the way a person sees self) is the same as the individual's biology (their body parts) the term used for that person's gender identity is cisgender. Most people are cisgender. A transgender individual does not identify with biology. There are many other words used to describe a person's gender. (genderqueer, bigendered) It's important not to confuse children. Again, less is more.

- Children may express their feelings about gender very early. Experts in the field of gender and psychology recommend that adults follow a child's lead when the subject is something as personal and sensitive as gender.

- As Tamika and Alex discover in the book, respect does not mean an individual likes another person. Even if you do not understand changes surrounding gender, or if your belief system discourages non-traditional gender expression, I hope you will be open-minded enough to teach your children respect for others.

- Each person is a person of worth. Please pass it on.

- Thank you.   *Mary Jo Podgurski*

Resources

Websites:

https://www.genderspectrum.org/

http://www.rollingstone.com/culture/news/about-a-girl-coy-mathis-fight-to-change-change-gender-20131028

http://childrensnational.org/files/PDF/DepartmentsAndPrograms/Neuroscience/Psychiatry/Gender VariantOutreachProgram/GVParentBrochure.pdf (Brochure by Children's National Health System)

time.com/135480/transgender-tipping-point

http://www.imatyfa.org/ Trans-Youth Family Allies

Books:

The Transgender Child by Stephanie Brill & Rachel Pepper
This comprehensive first of its kind guidebook explores the unique challenges that thousands of families face every day raising their children in every city and state.

Gender Born, Gender Made by Diane Ehrensaft, Ph.D.
Gender Born, Gender Made brings to our homes, schools and clinician's offices a wealth of ideas and tools that will prove invaluable as we move towards a more empathic, just and inclusive society.

You Tube:

There are many videos and documentaries on You Tube covering the experiences of families with transgender children.

    a. 20/20 - A Story of Transgender Children (https://www.youtube.com/watch?v=YfqmEYC_rMI)

    b. I am Jazz (http://abcnews.go.com/2020/video/transgender-11-jazzs-story-22507438)

    c. Becoming Me (Full Episode) (https://www.youtube.com/watch?v=IxzKlPVceWg)

    d. Living a Transgender Childhood (https://www.youtube.com/watch?v=oYOY1Clyd_0)

    e. The Whittington Family: Ryland's Story (https://www.youtube.com/watch?v=LcgFOYZDE5c)

    f. The documentary film Two Spirits is available at http://twospirits.org/

*Answers to the learning game on pg 49: 1= she; 2 = he; 3 =she; 4 = he; 5 = ze or they/them

Origins of the Grandmother Names on Page 9:

Abuela: Peru	Grams: U.S.	Some other names for grandmother:	People who speak Mandarin Chinese use a different name for a grandma on a child's mom's side of the family (po po) than a grandma on a child's dad's side of the family (gong gong).
Avo: Brazil	Maimeo: Ireland	Bomma: Belgium	
Awa: India	Oma: Germany	Bunica: Romania	
Babushka: Russia	Savta: Israel	Grandmere: France	
Bibi: Kenya	Shimasani: Navajo	Kuku: Hawaii	
Halmoni: Korea	Sobo: Japan	Lola: Philippines	
Jaddah: Morroco	Yaya: Greece	Nonna: Italy	
Gramma: U.S.		Pog: Laos	
		Yeay: Cambodia	

About the Author

Dr. Mary Jo Podgurski is the founder and director of The Washington Health System Teen Outreach and the Academy for Adolescent Health in Washington, Pa. She is a nurse, a counselor, a parent, a trainer and speaker, and an educator who is dedicated to serving young people. The Outreach has reached over 230,000 young people since 1988. Check out www.healthyteens.com for information on the Academy and its programs. Mary Jo's information is available at DrMaryJoPodgurski.com.

Dr. Podgurski is certified as a childbirth educator through Lamaze International, as a sexuality educator and a sexuality counselor through AASECT (American Associaton of Sexuality Educators, Counselors and Therapists), as an Olweus Bullying Prevention Program trainer and through Parents As Teachers. She is the author of the *Ask Mary Jo* weekly column in the Observer-Reporter newspaper and answers 6—10 questions from young people daily. Most important, Mary Jo and her partner Rich are the parents of three wonderful adult children and are blessed to be grandparents.

Interested in Nonnie Talks about Gender?

Nonnie Talks about Gender's goal is education and communication.
Dr. Podgurski has dedicated her life to both goals.
She is available for workshops and consultation. You can reach her at:

Email: podmj@healthyteens.com
Toll free #: 1 (888) 301-2311
Twitter: DrMaryJoPod

Made in the USA
Charleston, SC
19 March 2016